VIEW FROM THE FLIGHT DECK

FRONT COVER:
The airport of Malé, in the Maldive islands, is also known as 'the aircraft carrier in the Indian Ocean'. Located some 700 km (400 miles) south-west of Sri Lanka, it has become a favourite destination for travellers who are interested in snorkelling and diving. Flight time from Europe is around ten hours. The runway is 3,200 metres long and has instrument approach facilities. A seaplane base is located directly next to the runway.

BACK COVER:
Another day at the office at 33,000 feet over the Libyan desert in January 1998. I should like to thank all of you who find interest in this volume, and hope that you enjoy the wide variety of aircraft, locations selected and the unusual views from the flight deck.

VIEW FROM THE FLIGHT DECK

Detmar Härter

Airlife

First published in the UK in 2002
by Airlife Publishing Ltd

British Library Cataloguing-in-Publication Data
        A catalogue record for this book
        is available from the British Library

ISBN 1 84037 324 5

Printed in Hong Kong

For a complete list of all Airlife titles please contact:
Airlife Publishing Ltd
101 Longden Road, Shrewsbury, SY3 9EB, England
E-mail: sales@airlifebooks.com
Website: www.airlifebooks.com

OPPOSITE:
The classic cockpit layout (with its hydromechanical instruments and the T-shape basic configuration of the essential airspeed, horizon and altimeter) of an aircraft generation that has lasted for more than fifty years, and will continue to be used, despite shrinking numbers, for at least another twenty-five years! This picture features the workplace of a Middle East Airlines Boeing 707 crew during ground time at Geneva in May 1990. The engine indicators showing engine pressure ratio, compressor speeds and fuel flow are clearly visible. A single weather radar is installed underneath, framed by two inertial reference system navigation computers. MEA still owns this aircraft eleven years later, but it is stored at Beirut and waiting for a new operator.

INTRODUCTION

Aviation and photography are two passions truly enjoyed by many people around the world. *View from the Flight Deck* is a new book written by an airline pilot for aviation enthusiasts. All these pictures have been selected from my private collection of around 5,000 photographs that I have taken in the past twelve years of worldwide airline operation. All have been taken with Canon cameras and Fuji film. The action covers every angle of modern jet flying, from runway shots to high-level encounters in the skies around the globe. So, sit back, relax and enjoy the flight.

Airbus introduced a revolutionary design with its new-generation family in 1987. The missing control column and fly-by-wire concept initiated heated discussions among airline pilots worldwide. Today it has become routine. More than half of all switches, toggles, circuit breakers and lights have been shelved in favour of six flat screens. Two primary flight displays, two navigation displays, an engine warning display and a system display provide all the information needed in normal and abnormal conditions. Electronic checklists are incorporated, in addition to the latest technology of enhanced terrain avoidance, traffic alerts and multi-colour weather radars. The technical status of hydraulics, fuel, electrics, flight controls and pneumatic systems can be selected upon request on the lower screen. Illustrated here is the flight deck of an Airbus 330-300 series aircraft.

This Douglas DC-10-30 aircraft, belonging to African Safari Airways, uses 'Zebra'as its callsign. Founded in l968, ASA used DC-8-33 and -53 series, a -63 was leased intermittently, to fly tourists, on behalf of the tour operator African Safari Club, from destinations in Switzerland and Germany to Kenya.

Tourism was booming by that time, and many hotels on the Diani Beach and around Malindi were built during the early 1970s, providing sufficient business for the new carrier. Photographed here on the tarmac in Mombasa is the company's sole aircraft, 5Y-MBA. Since MBA is the three-letter identification

code for Mombasa, a more appropriate registration was not possible! The aircraft was delivered new to KLM in February 1975, as PH-DTL (ln185/msn46592). The aircraft has recently been sold to Africa One and is being replaced by an ex-Hapag-Lloyd Airbus 310.

Resting on the ramp in Düsseldorf, Germany, is this Condor DC-10-30. Delivered new to Lufthansa's charter subsidiary in 1979, the aircraft was heavily used on the company's worldwide network, covering the Mediterranean, USA, Africa, the Caribbean and some isolated places in the Indian Ocean. With the arrival of the Boeing 757 and 767, Condor retired its last DC-10 in 1999. In addition to the Boeing fleet, the company employs twelve Airbus 320s, mostly on flights to sunny destinations around Spain and Greece. The DC-10s have been operated in a single-class, 370-seat configuration and are powered by three General Electric CF-6 series engines.

Since France historically has many overseas *départements*, the DC-10 turned out to be the perfect aircraft to link Paris with ultra-long-haul destinations like New Caledonia, Tahiti, Réunion, Mauritius and the French Antilles. The routes to the South Pacific are flown either westbound, via Los Angeles, or eastbound with stops in Colombo and Sydney. AOM, formerly known as Air Outre Mer, merged with Minerve, which also operated the DC-10 by that time, on 1 March 1992. Captured on the ramp in Arrecife, Canary Islands, in August 1998 is F-GTDI (ln77/msn46890). Built in 1973 and delivered to Air Afrique as TU-TAL, this aircraft was destroyed in a tragic landing accident at Guatemala City on 21 December 1999, when it was on lease to Cubana.

'All lights on, cleared to land 24R.' Moments from touchdown in Los Angeles is this Hawaiian DC-10-30 after completion of the 5½hr trip from Honolulu. Founded in 1929, Hawaiian is one of the oldest airlines in the world. A long-time Douglas customer, Hawaiian uses a large number of DC-9 aircraft on local services around the Hawaiian islands. Since these all date from the mid-1970s, the airline is going to replace them with Boeing 717s, starting in 2001. The evaluation process of the DC-10 replacement is under way as well, with the Boeing 767 turning out to be the front-runner.

Eyed by two DC-10s, operated by American and Hawaiian respectively, we are taxiing eastbound, parallel to Runway 25R at Los Angeles International Airport (also known as LAX) after an exhausting 11¾ hr trip from Germany. Since our gate was 119 that day, located on the northern side of the International building, we had to taxi all the way up to the other side of the airport. Despite the fact that taxiing at LAX has been simplified by prescribed routes, blocked gates can cause a massive delay, and often result in reclearances to remote parking stands.

'Airborne' at Palma de Mallorca on another no-frills, low-cost flight to London-Luton Airport is easyJet's Boeing 737-375, G-EZYF, featuring the company's direct-booking hot-line number on the fuselage. Founded by Greek entrepreneur Stelios Haji-Ioannou, easyJet entered a market in Europe that was yet to be exploited. With its American counterpart Southwest as inspiration, easyJet is one of Europe's fastest-growing airlines. With sixteen -300 series and seven 700s already in service, and another 32 B 737-700s on order, easyJet will become a frequent visitor to many European airports. The paint scheme will differ from one aircraft to another slightly, but will mainly comprise the company's Internet address on later models.

On a positioning flight from Frankfurt to San Francisco on board a Lufthansa Boeing 747-230, we were crossing Greenland on a magnificently clear day, without any cloud formation covering the everlasting ice and snow. Flying over Greenland entails thorough planning in case, for example, of the unlikely event of loss of cabin pressure.

The country's mountains and ice shelves reach an average of over 3,300 metres (15,000 feet), so any diversion has to be executed with great care, especially at night-time. It covers an area of 2,200,000 sq. km (840,000 sq. miles). The flight time from Frankfurt to San Francisco averages eleven hours.

Entering the flight deck of a Boeing 767-300ER at night affords an impressive sight. With a light check just being conducted, it looks even more fascinating. These checks are done on the ground, prior to leaving the gate, to test all annunciator lights are functioning correctly. The different colours indicate the priority level of the failed system.

A direct view from the first officer's seat during sunrise. Clearly visible in the centre of the picture are the standby instruments – the artificial horizon at the top, then the airspeed indicator and the altimeter. In case all electronics, and therefore the essential attitude and navigation data produced from a modern flight management system, are lost, the pilots are still able to return to the absolute basics. The gear lever, on the right, has been placed in the off position to depressurize the system, a common procedure on all Boeing aircraft.

With 8:02 hrs elapsed flying time on the clock and cruising at Mach 0.82, we are reaching Ireland in the early dawn in February 1998, on our return from Cuba. The route that night was more or less parallel to the eastern seaboard of the United States, controlled by the various air traffic control centres, before being handed over to Gander Center, in Canadian airspace, which issues the North Atlantic clearances and controls the North Atlantic region up to 30 degrees west. Thereafter you are in the hands of Shanwick Oceanic, with a pick-up from the first radar controller in Shannon, Ireland. Subsequently we were handed over to London Centre, Maastricht Control, Amsterdam Radar and finally Düsseldorf Radar, which provided us with radar vectors to the final approach course.

Returning to the classics! This shot was taken on board a Sabre B 727-200 series aircraft on the ground in Faro, Portugal, in December 1997. Before the modern glass cockpit was invented, everything was in the hands of the flight engineer. With his seat turned 90 degrees facing 'the panel', any switch or button was within reach. The main engine instruments were located on the forward centre panel, just underneath the three fire handles. With only a few passenger B 727s left in Europe, this view will become very rare in the near future.

Cruising 3,000 feet higher and a little faster than us is a B 747-436 of British Airways in the early morning hours of 5 May 1999, coming home from another long-haul mission. BA uses its 747s, powered by four Rolls-Royce RB 211-524H2 engines, on an extensive worldwide network, covering more than 170 destinations on all continents. Employing the -400 series since June 1989, BA still has fifteen classic -200s in its fleet, along with 57 -400s. With the classics being phased out in the near future, the carrier is switching to the more economical Boeing 777. Although a long-time all-Boeing customer, BA has also placed a massive order for the Airbus 318/319/320 fleet to replace its B 737 fleet, a surprise to the aircraft industry.

Founded in 1972, by the traditional Hapag-Lloyd shipping company, this airline operated with three Boeing 727-100s to destinations around the Mediterranean. With the merger of Hapag-Lloyd and Bavaria/Germanair in 1978, the first set of Airbus 300B4s joined the fleet. Subsequently they were replaced by Airbus 310 models, as the B 727s were exchanged for B 737s. The Airbus 310 was also briefly used on some long-haul trips from Germany to the Dominican Republic. Today Hapag-Lloyd has seven B 737-400s, 25 B 737-800s and six A310s in its fleet, with a successor being sought for the last model. On climbout from Palma de Mallorca, on an early morning departure back to its Hannover home base, is D-AHLC, which was leased new to Hapag-Lloyd in 1992.

Pushing back from the gate in Colombo, Sri Lanka, and getting ready for its 4½hr trip to Doha is an Airbus 300-622R belonging to Qatar Airways, on lease from Ansett Worldwide Aviation Service. The Airbus 300 family has become very popular in the Middle East, as several other airlines, such as Emirates, Kuwait Airways, Royal Jordanian, Saudi and Iran Air also use the wide-body aircraft to carry their passengers around the region. Qatar Airways has four of the type, along with six Airbus 320s and a single A340-211, which is used as a VIP aircraft by the government. The three remaining B 727-200s are currently on sale.

Waiting for its next night-time rotation out of Athens, in the heat of a June morning in 1998, is this Airbus A300B4-103F, PH-EAN, operated by the Dutch carrier Farnair on behalf of DHL. The worldwide operating express courier uses, next to its own DC-8s and B 727s, which mainly operate in the United States, a large fleet of chartered aircraft from its principal hubs in Europe. Leaving the gateways in Brussels, East Midlands and Cologne every night, the Airbus 300B4 can carry up to 40 tons over a range of 3,500 km (2,175 miles). Pictured here is an early model from 1977, which originally operated with Eastern Airlines as N201EA.

Middle East Airlines recently changed its old colours for this almost white livery, featuring the traditional cedar tree on the vertical fin. The history of MEA goes back to 1945 when it started its initial service with three Dragon Rapide aircraft. Since that time MEA has had alliances with several major carriers, including Pan Am and Air France. Aircraft types changed frequently until 1968, with the arrival of the first Boeing 707, which was still used in the 1990s. Owing to the long-lasting civil war in Lebanon, the carrier battled hard all those years, with several aircraft being destroyed during bomb raids on Beirut. This ex-Singapore Airlines A310-222 joined the Lebanese carrier's fleet during a period of expansion. Registered in Mauritius as 3B-STI, the Airbus taxies out of the main ramp in Larnaca, Cyprus, in the evening twilight of May 1999 for a short twenty-minute sortie to neighbouring Beirut. The airline's callsign is 'Cedarjet'!

Arriving at the Maldive islands from Vienna, via Dubai, is a representative of the Austrian flag carrier. Comprising a mixed fleet of Airbus 310/320/330 and 340 aircraft, as well some MD-87s and Fokker 70 jets, Austrian Airlines recently broke its ties with Swissair and joined the Star Alliance Group led by Lufthansa and United. Strongly orientated to Eastern European destinations, Austrian also serves New York, Tokyo, Johannesburg and the major capitals all over Europe. Coming onto the ramp is an Airbus 310-324, OE-LAC, named after the city of Paris. This particular plane is no longer with the company, probably partly because it was the only aircraft in the A310 fleet that did not have any first-class seats. The seating arrangement was 49 coach and 123 economy.

Another new airline founded in Egypt is Pharaoh Airlines. Using two Boeing 737s, a -200 and a -400 series, which is spotted here on the ramp in Luxor, Southern Egypt, the carrier connects Hurghada, Sharm el Sheik and Luxor with its home base, the capital of Egypt, Cairo. Brief charter flights to Europe are also undertaken to carry holiday-makers to the sunny beaches of the Red Sea. The sandy colour scheme of the fuselage perfectly complements the desert surroundings of Egypt. Note the Pharaoh mask on the vertical fin.

Roaring through the blue sky over southern California into Los Angeles is N706AS, a B 737-490 belonging to Alaska Airlines. As Alaska Airlines' home base is in Seattle it is perhaps not surprising that it is a major customer of Boeing. With 67 Boeing 737s already in service, mainly -400 and -700 series aircraft, Alaska was the launch customer for Boeing's latest derivative, the -900. This stretched B 737, the longest ever built, will accommodate 177 passengers in Alaska's configuration, and took to the air in May 2001. The aircraft will be operated between Seattle, Los Angeles, Phoenix, Las Vegas and Anchorage.

When the first Boeing 737 took to the air on 9 April 1967, surely nobody predicted that this type, with the various versions to follow, would become the most successful airliner ever built. They are still in production 35 years later, with thousands of them delivered worldwide. This classic -200 series aircraft from Air Tanzania, 5H-ATC, was built in 1978 and has been cruising over Africa ever since. Linking Dar es Salaam with Mombasa every morning, the aircraft is a regular visitor to Kenya, where this shot was taken in June 1997. Powered by 'Jet Noise' JT-8D-17 engines, this aircraft will fly for many more years to come over Africa, where noise regulations are not so common as in other parts of the world.

Dawn over the Bay of Bengal in October 1995, en route from Abu Dhabi to Bangkok. We are some 400 miles south of Chittagong, Bangladesh, and approaching the boundary of Myanmar, formerly Burma. The remaining flight time is a little more than one hour. Flying in this part of the world is pretty interesting, since most of the flying is done outside radar coverage and any VHF radio contact for the majority of the routes. Old short-wave communication procedures are in effect, resulting in a megamix of position reports from many aircraft talking to the respective radio station at the same time. Because of the direct effect of sunlight, owing to the changing ionosphere, which in turn reflects the radio waves going into space, short-wave communication is difficult during sunrise and sunset conditions.

Long-haul operations are a unique challenge. Depending on the company's network and the aircraft type involved, you might end up in any corner of the globe: from the tropics to the desert, from the heat of a big city to an isolated island; crossing the Arctic Ocean or the Sahara Desert; penetrating the Inter-tropical Convergence Zone (ITC) or fighting the magnificent thunderclouds that develop during the hurricane and typhoon season. With more and more twin-engined aircraft, like the Boeing 767/777 and the Airbus 330, deployed on long-range flights, another aspect has come up – extended twin-engine operations (ETOPS). Regulations require a twin-engined aircraft to reach a suitable airport, in case of an engine shutdown in flight, within 60, 120 or 180 minutes. Certain operators already have approval to dispatch with a 207-minute diversion time, to cover routes via the Pacific. The granted diversion time depends on the reliability of the airline and aircraft/ engine type involved. In the early days of long-range flights, arctic or tropical survival equipment was carried on board, in the event of a forced landing in remote areas. With airframes and engines becoming more and more reliable, those items have been removed. Navigation equipment is being progressively enhanced, with earlier means of navigation by Loran and Omega systems ditched almost completely, and succeeded by Inertial Reference Systems and Global Positioning.

This photograph shows us on short final to the desert runway of Hurghada, Egypt. The temperature was almost 40°C (104°F) when we landed during a technical stop en route from Mombasa to Düsseldorf in June 1999. Prevailing headwinds on the northbound leg from Africa towards Europe make refuelling necessary in a B 757.

One of the most interesting and challenging approaches can be made into Funchal, Madeira, where this Boeing 737-3Q8 was captured on its take-off run in February 1998. With the particular location of the runway, right below a hillside, certain wind conditions from the north-west make it virtually impossible to get the aircraft onto the deck because of severe turbulence and windshear on the very short final. Since the runway length was only about 1,500 metres until mid-2000, when it was lengthened to almost 2,800 metres, it was necessary to touch down at the near end. So diversions to the neighbouring island of Porto Santo or Tenerife were quite common. Special pilot training to operate into Madeira is required from the Portuguese authorities. Departing here for Ponta Delgada, in the Azores, is a SATA International aircraft, linking mainland Portugal with its dependent islands in the Atlantic.

Northwest's relations with the Douglas factory are nearly as old as both companies. Formerly known as Northwest Orient, the carrier was one of the pioneers on long-distance flights from the USA to the Far East, crossing the Pacific and the North Pole with DC-4 aircraft. Bigger and faster DC-6, -7, -8, -9 and finally -10s, followed. Taxiing out to the active runway at Phoenix Sky Harbour International Airport is N151US (ln120/msn46760), a DC-10-40. Northwest Orient ordered the first batch of fourteen DC-10s in late 1968, originally dubbed the -20 series owing to the fact that the aircraft was powered by P&W JT-9-20D engines. Prior to the first delivery it was renumbered the -40 series. Northwest still has 22 -30 series and 21 -40 series planes employed on its current network.

American was the launch customer, with United, for the DC-10 in 1972, with ship number 1 handed over, in a big ceremony, at the Long Beach plant. The -10 and -15 series aircraft have a slightly smaller wingspan than the -30 and -40 series aircraft, resulting in a reduction of fuel capacity and therefore less range than their intercontinental counterparts. American mainly uses them on trans-USA services, connecting major cities like New York, Miami, Dallas and Los Angeles, where high capacity is needed. N168AA (ln153/msn46938) is seen descending into Los Angeles. Originally delivered to Western in May 1974, this DC-10-10 series aircraft has been in service with several other airlines, such as Capitol, Air Hawaii, Pacific East and The Hawaii Express. Note the missing centre gear, a clear indication of the -10 series.

This Air Atlanta wet-lease wears the colours of the British tour operator Peach Air, a joint venture between Caledonian Airways and Goldcrest Aviation. This L-1011-1 series, TF-ABH, was seen in Tenerife-South during the summer of 1998. It was powered by Rolls-Royce RB-211-22B powerplants, the British engine manufacturer being the sole supplier to the L-1011 programme. With Rolls-Royce struggling financially later on and the British government not willing to pump money into the company, Lockheed was ready to jump in with help from Washington. By that time, Lockheed had already lost the battle against its rival McDonnell-Douglas, with its DC-10 project, despite the fact that the safety record of the L-1011 later turned out to be outstanding. This aircraft is an ex-Cathay Pacific model – VR-HHX.

While we are waiting for our line-up clearance to depart on Runway 04 at Colombo Bandaranaike International Airport on the 10½hr flight to Europe, AirLanka's TriStar 4R-ULE burns the rubber, inbound on the early morning run from Singapore. This converted -50 series airframe is an ex-All Nippon aircraft, JA8503. Launched in September 1979, from the remains of Air Ceylon, AirLanka started flying with a Boeing 707, 4R-ALA, leased from Singapore Airlines. One year later the first L-1011 aircraft joined it, and international services to Paris, London and Frankfurt were increased. Two Boeing 747s followed later, but were found to be too large and were returned to their lessor, Qantas. Traditionally linked deeply with tea and garment export, AirLanka connects all major Asian cities, such as Bangkok, Kuala Lumpur, Hong Kong and Singapore, as well as Sydney, with the island of Sri Lanka. With the retirement of the last L-1011 in 1999 and Emirates now having a major stake, the airline's name was changed to SriLankan. The present fleet exists purely of Airbus 320, 330 and 340 aircraft.

Roaring into the heated sky of Miami in July 1998 is this L-1011-500 series, SE-DVI, belonging to Swedish carrier Novair. With the landing gear in transit, which has to carry a maximum take-off weight of 231,300 kg, the long-range -500 series is bound for Stockholm. The latest and shortest variant of the TriStar family made its maiden flight on 16 October 1978. Following an initial order for this variant by British Airways, two more European carriers joined the club, TAP from Portugal and LTU from Germany. Royal Jordanian became a big player in the Middle East, with one aircraft being used as a state aircraft by the late King Hussein, which he piloted on certain occasions as well. This particular aircraft, JY-HKJ, is the lowest-time L-1011 that is currently on the market. With the fuselage a little more than 4 metres (13 feet) shorter, and the wingspan increased by 2.6 metres (8.5 feet), the -500 is easy to recognize.

Inbound to Frankfurt, in the late evening hours in July 1997, is an Atlas Air B 747-200 Cargo returning from Nairobi on behalf of Lufthansa Cargo. The flower trunk route to the east African country is so lucrative that Lufthansa did not have enough cargo planes at that time to fulfil all contracts, and so wet-leased aircraft had to be employed. Starting its own full cargo service in 1977, called German Cargo Services, Lufthansa operated four B 707-320Fs initially on routes to the Far East, with intermediate stops, mostly in Dubai and Karachi. South America was later added to the agenda, as well as various destinations like Lagos, Harare, Djibouti, Nairobi and Johannesburg. One B 707F, D-ABUY, was tragically lost on 26 July 1979 during climbout departing Rio de Janeiro.

The Boeing aircraft were later replaced by DC-8-73Fs, with the initial batch provided by Cargolux. With a restructuring of Lufthansa in 1995, the cargo arm was renamed Lufthansa Cargo. The DC-8s were sold to the United States and replaced by new MD-11 freighters. Today Lufthansa Cargo operates ten B 747-230Fs and fourteen MD-11Fs, with the last ever built MD-11 handed over to the German carrier in spring 2001!

Originally built as a TriStar -1 series aircraft in 1974, G-BBAJ, named *Loch Rannoch*, was later converted into a -100 series. In 1987 British Airways bought British Caledonian and formed, with its own charter affiliate British Airtours, Caledonian. Carrying British sun-seekers to a variety of places in the Mediterranean with Boeing 737 aircraft, which came from British Airtours, the wide-body L-1011s were mainly used on high trunk routes to the Canary Islands as well as long-haul flights to the Caribbean and Kenya. The Boeing 737 was subsequently replaced by the Airbus 320. Two DC-10-30 series aircraft joined the fleet later. Owing to massive changes in the European charter business, especially in Britain and Germany, Caledonian left the scene when it was merged with another nearly-new British company, Flying Colours, which is illustrated in this book later (see page 94). The new company name is JMC. The location of this shot is Abu Dhabi in April 1999, as *Lord Rannoch* taxies out to Runway 31, after heavy maintenance checks have been carried out by the local specialist GAMCO.

If money is not an issue and you want to buy a VIP aircraft, the Boeing 747SP is the number one choice of a lot of rulers around the world, especially in the Middle East! Equipped with everything from large dining areas, conference rooms and dressing rooms with a shower, to a communication centre and medical facilities is this B 747SP (ln329/msn21652) resting on the ramp in Malaga, southern Spain. Built for His Majesty King Khalid of Saudi Arabia, it left the Boeing plant in July 1979 registered HZ-HM1. Since that time the aircraft has flown fewer than 4,000 hours, which is considered still brand-new. There are only two B 747SPs which have even fewer hours. These belong to the governments of Iraq (ln567/msn22858), YI-ALM, and Abu Dhabi (ln676/msn23610), A6-ZSN. When King Fahd of Saudi Arabia received his larger B 747-3G1 it was registered HZ-HM1A, so subsequently the smaller SP had to be reregistered HZ-HM1B, its current tail number. For safety reasons the aircraft belonging to the Royal Family are painted in the airline livery.

Pushing back in Zurich on a rainy summer day in 1999 is JA8089, a B 747-446 from Japan Airlines. With only American-made aircraft in its inventory, JAL is the largest Boeing 747 operator in the world. It has no fewer than 91 B 747s, including five -100s, 23 -200s, thirteen -300s and 50 -400s, in every kind of variant, since freighter, domestic and international versions are employed! High-density versions are used on the traditional inner Japanese trunk routes such as Tokyo–Osaka or Nagoya–Sapporo. The -400 passenger version, with its stretched upper deck and newly developed winglets, is the easiest to distinguish from the -300; however, the domestic versions, which only fly with Japanese airlines, do not have winglets, contributing to a lot of confusion among aircraft enthusiasts. JA8089 was the 905th Jumbo built when it was rolled out in March 1992.

Challenge Air Cargo of Miami took delivery of the first of three DC-10-40F aircraft in September 1998. All the aircraft were previously operated by Japan Airlines. Seen here on final approach into Miami is N141WE, returning from a trip to Latin America. A single Boeing 757PF is used for destinations where the cargo volume is not sufficient to fill a DC-10. Founded in 1985, the company used some ex-Lufthansa Boeing 707s in the very lucrative 40-ton payload perishable segment of freight operation linking Colombia, Guatemala, Panama, Honduras, Dominican Republic and Ecuador with the United States. Ad hoc charters are also undertaken on behalf of several freight forwarders located in the Miami area. Now controlled by UPS, it keeps its own identity. Its callsign is 'Challenge Cargo'.

The hadj season is one of the more interesting times during the year for photographing new or mixed paint schemes. One example is captured here as it docks at the stand in Düsseldorf in April 1998. Wearing Saudia's basic tail scheme (now known as Saudi Arabian Airlines), it is in fact an Air Atlanta B 747-246B, TF-ABY, which is used to fly pilgrims between Germany and Jeddah, in Saudi Arabia. The aircraft formerly belonged to Japan Airlines and is configured in a single 476 seating layout. A tremendous number of Muslims fly each year during the holy period to Mecca, mainly departing Lagos, Kano in Nigeria, Dhaka in Bangladesh, Jakarta in Indonesia and certain cities in Europe. To cope with that demand the home carriers of those countries, like Saudi and Garuda Indonesia, charter additional wide-body capacity from the wet-lease specialists. Wet lease, the term that has been used in this book several times, indicates that a flight deck and/or cabin crew is chartered as well on the particular contract. TF-ABY (ln251/msn21030) left the Boeing company in 1974 and was previously registered as JA8125. The engines are four Pratt & Whitney JT-9Ds.

You cannot get any closer to a Boeing 747 in flight unless you are on a special photo flight or conducting an intercept mission in a military jet! Vertical separation was reduced to 1,000 feet (300 metres) over the north Atlantic, in February 2001, when we met this Air France B 747-228B, F-GCBB, which was en route to Saint Maarten in the Lesser Antilles, in the Caribbean. The French flag carrier was founded in 1933, initially using equipment from Aérospatiale and Breguet. Routes to Africa were inaugurated, linking the controlled territories of the Central African Republic, Chad, Ivory Coast and Cameroon with Paris. Using B 707, and later B 747, aircraft cut travel time to isolated islands in the South Pacific, like Tahiti and New Caledonia, significantly. When the independent French carrier UTA was acquired in 1992, the first DC-10 and B 747-300 aircraft joined the fleet, with the Douglas trijet no longer in operation with Air France.

Formed in 1989, EVA Air, a member of the Evergreen shipping group, has been growing significantly over the years, with its current fleet totalling 38 wide-body aircraft. Having its own fleet of cargo ships, freight has become a vital element of the Taiwan-based airline, which uses nine MD-11F and three B 747-400F aircraft, with the majority of the passenger 747s being combi versions. Spotted here is B-16109 as it taxies to the cargo ramp in Los Angeles, arriving from Taipei after an intermediate stop in Anchorage. This aircraft joined the fleet in December 1997. MD-11s have become successful cargo aircraft, the bulk of them being operated by FedEx and Lufthansa Cargo. Prices for second-hand passenger models have risen sharply since these planes are sought for cargo conversion. The last MD-11 ever built was handed over to Lufthansa Cargo in spring 2001.

There are many types of desert in the world, from sandy, with some intermittent vegetation, to rockstone-type formations, as in the Omani desert near Muscat.

The Boeing 707 was approaching the end of its production run, after more than twenty years, and Boeing came up with a radical new design, developed simultaneously with the B 757, a six-abreast twin-engined wide-body, capable of replacing the four-engined classic on all routes in terms of range and payload. The first B 767-200 soared into the sky over Seattle on 26 September 1981 – five months earlier than its smaller sister, the B 757. Cockpit commonality was a major goal for Boeing, anticipating that potential customer airlines would buy both types, so enabling their pilots to operate two aircraft with one type-rating. It worked out, and more or less all airlines, except a few like Kuwait Airways, Air Mauritius and Varig, ordered both types. The Boeing 767-200 became very popular in the Middle East and Africa, leading to numerous world records being broken almost weekly during delivery flights from the USA to the customer home bases.

One of these record-setting aircraft is featured here as it taxies into Frankfurt in February 1998. B 767-2Q8ER, S 7-AAS, was delivered on 27 July 1989 from Seattle to Grand Rapids, Michigan, and then non-stop over a distance of 14,300 km (7,720 nm) to the Seychelles, in the Indian Ocean.

New York! En route to Florida we were crossing the 'Big Apple' on a beautiful sunny day right over Manhattan. Clearly visible are Central Park, Wall Street to the left, Brooklyn, Manhattan and Williamsburg Bridge in the lower left corner. The Hudson and East River separate Manhattan from Newark, New Jersey, Brooklyn and Queens. The line in Frank Sinatra's famous song, 'I want to wake up in a city that doesn't sleep . . .' becomes reality with more than eight million people living here, another seventeen million in the area and the same number of tourists coming to New York every year! Famous theatres, operas, the Empire State Building or Broadway – New York offers everything and really is a place to visit. From the pilot's point of view, John F. Kennedy Airport is a challenge. Unbelievable traffic and fascinating approaches over Jamaica Bay are conducted by instructions from extremely professional air traffic controllers.

Trans World Airlines is a pioneer of American aviation history, without any doubt. Based in St Louis, Missouri, and dating back to 1930, under its original name of Transcontinental and Western Air, the carrier led the industry in many ways. It inaugurated coast-to-coast flights and crossed the Atlantic with connecting services to the Middle and Far East, always using the latest aviation technology that was available at the time. In 1950 the company changed its name to Trans World Airlines – TWA. Being one of the first carriers to introduce the B 707, B 747 and L-1011 TriStar, TWA ordered the B 767-200 in 1979 and was once again one of the first to put it into service. Financial difficulties arose in the early 1990s, forcing the carrier to raise fresh money and change its fleet policy. The L-1011 and the B 747 are no longer used. In fact, TWA operated the highest-time B 747-100 in the world, before disposing of it. TWA became another victim of deregulation in aviation, and it was merged into American Airlines in 2001. Pictured here is a B 767-231ER at Milan-Malpensa in March 1998, wearing the latest colour scheme.

Engines at idle produce almost enough thrust for this All Nippon B 747-481 to leave the ramp and taxi out to Runway 25 in Frankfurt, for another 10½hr night flight back to Tokyo. ANA is Japan's second largest international carrier, also operating a large number of wide-body aircraft, including 55 B 767-200 and -300 series, 26 B 777-200s and -300s with another three on order, fifteen B 747-281s and 23 B 747-481s! Another nine B 747-200 cargo aircraft fly for the subsidiary Nippon Cargo Airlines. All

Nippon's engine choice for the B 747 and B 767 was the powerful General Electric CF-6-80 version, while the B 777s are powered by the dependable Pratt & Whitney 4000 series. The modern flight deck of the -400 allows the aircraft to be flown by two pilots, eliminating the flight engineer's panel, but because of duty time regulations all B 747-400s are flown with at least three or four pilots, and even up to six, on the long sectors.

Flying at 37,000 feet, we are still way below the top of this massive cloud formation near Libreville, Gabon, in the summer of 1994. Crossing the equatorial region in Africa, especially in the western part of the continent, is accompanied by diversions around weather, sometimes fifty or sixty miles away from the original track.

After the successful introduction of the 767-200 series, Boeing decided to stretch the aircraft by 6.41 metres and increase the range by additional fuel capacity. Known as the B 767-300 (and ER) model, the aircraft became an even bigger seller than its shorter sister. Initial delivery was in September 1985 to Japan Airlines, with the ER extended-range version handed over to American Airlines a year later. Gulf Air, British Airways, All Nippon, SAS, EVA Air and leasing companies followed subsequently with large orders. With more and more twin-engined aircraft employed over long-distance flights, the B 767-300ER has become the number one aircraft over the Atlantic – something that ten to fifteen years ago, when the 3- and 4-engined wide-bodies were dominating the North Atlantic, was unthinkable. High popularity with European charter carriers makes the B 767-300ER the standard long-haul aircraft for many companies, including Eurofly. The charter arm of Alitalia has three -300ER series in service, with EI-CRD being the first one delivered, in October 1998, and photographed three months later taxiing down the runway in Malé, arriving after a night flight from Milan.

The first officer's instrument panel of a Boeing 767-300ER is illustrated here. Seen upper left, is the airspeed indicator. Because of the erroneous indication of airspeed at high levels, modern jet aircraft are flown by Mach number. Here we are cruising at almost 82 per cent of the speed of sound. The white 'bugs' are still left on the take-off-decision and flap-retraction speeds. Hence the minimum speed, without deploying any slats or flaps, is 252 knots, clearly indicating a heavy-weight take-off this morning. Visible top centre

is the ADI (better known as the horizon). Wings are kept level by the autopilot, with the autothrust, vertical and lateral navigation modes engaged, indicated by the green modes in the lower part of the screen. The altimeter is top right. Cruising at 31,000 feet (9,450 metres), it is set to the standard barometric pressure of 1,013 millibars, or 29.92 inches of mercury. To make sure that all aircraft get the correct vertical separation, this setting is used above the so-called transition altitude, which varies from country to country.

In Germany, for example, it is 5,000 feet, and in the United States 18,000 feet. The lower left instrument gives us bearing and distance information to selected navigation aids on the ground. With the HSI or horizontal situation indicator (lower middle) selected for map mode, navigation is initially done by means of the pre-entered routeing from the flight management computer. One of the most important (believe it or not) instruments, in any type of aircraft, is the clock, lower right. Here it shows 10:11 GMT and 1:05 hours elapsed time of flight.

The Arctic Sea! The aircraft's present position is 80 degrees north and 130 degrees west. Departing Anchorage bound for Europe led us via Fairbanks onto Deadhorse and further northwards to a maximum latitude of 85 degrees north, bringing us to within 300 nautical miles of the North Pole! A fixed routeing system is established between the arctic region and Europe, called the Polar Track System. Track No. 4 was received in the clearance this day, which brought us directly towards Trondheim, Norway. Navigation in the polar region requires a different method owing to unreliable compass readings as a result of magnetic variations.

Faded Laker Airways was the inspiration for Sir Richard Branson, who made his money with Virgin Records, to found an airline in 1984 named Virgin Atlantic. Initially he used a single B 747-100 on the classic route between London and New York, and a second aircraft was added in 1986. Moving away from the no-frills status very quickly, increasing in-flight service and adding more attractive destinations, Virgin Atlantic has become a major player on the long-haul sector out of England. Today the company flies regular services to Hong Kong, Johannesburg, Tokyo, Sydney, Orlando, Chicago, Bangkok, Los Angeles and Miami. The fleet size has risen sharply to ten A340-300s, with ten A340-600s and six A380s on order. One of their B 747-400s, G-VTOP, is captured here on its final descent into Miami in July 1999.

With almost twenty years of production, more than a thousand delivered and no end in sight, the Boeing 757 has a remarkable safety record. In all those years just four aircraft have been written off. Performance has also not been beaten by any other single-aisle twin jet in its category, contributing to massive sales to European charter carriers, which also use the aircraft on thin long-haul routes to the Caribbean and on to the Far East.

The New York–Los Angeles route became possible with the B 757, eliminating the technical stops halfway along the route at the congested hubs in Minneapolis, Denver or Dallas, depending on which carrier you had chosen.

With no need to cross the continent in the early years of operation, America West Airlines started operations with six Boeing 737-200 series in 1983. Initial routes connected Phoenix with Las Vegas, Reno, Los Angeles and San Francisco. Passenger numbers grew, and bigger aircraft were needed, leading the way for the B 757-200. Departing Phoenix for Seattle is N913AW in the company's old livery in March 1998. This particular aircraft is one of the oldest B 757s in service (ln35/msn22207), and used to fly with launch customer Eastern Airlines as N517EA until operations ceased in 1992.

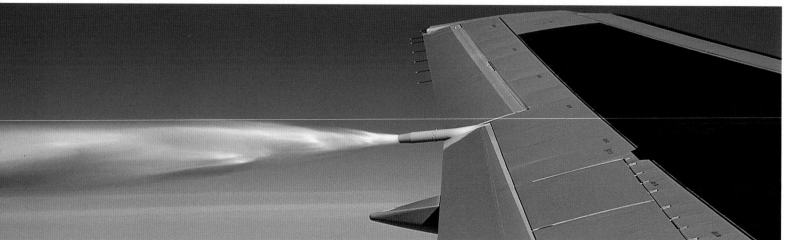

If you are travelling as a passenger and see this, you definitely know there is something wrong. Fuel dumping in progress! This dramatic shot was taken in October 1998, during an acceptance flight of a Boeing 767-300ER, in the Seattle area. All aircraft that are delivered new have to undergo thorough tests and checks before finally being handed over to the customer. Those checks are normally conducted by pilots from the customer airline involved and from the manufacturer, in this case Boeing, with some technicians travelling along as well. Starting on the ground, checking all lights, flight controls, hydraulics, high-speed take-off aborts and so on, you take the aircraft to the air for the first time. Once in the air you start with a series of stalls, lowering the flaps by alternative means, drop out all oxygen masks, cut all engines (one at a time, of course) and start them again. Then we came to the fuel jettison system, and since I had not seen that in real life, I left the cockpit to check it visually! Flow rate on a Boeing 767 is around 2,000 litres per minute. Fuel dumping is used in case of an immediate return, after a heavy-weight take-off, when conditions require it. For example, if you lose an engine or a medical emergency suddenly arises, and the runway length and/or conditions are not suitable for the weight of the aircraft.

Receiving final preparations before delivery in September 1998 is LanChile's first B 767-314ER freighter, CC-CZZ, on the ramp at Everett, featuring the carrier's striking new colour scheme. The company's DC-8-71F looks even better in the new paint scheme! Founded in 1929, LanChile is to the oldest operator from South America that offers B 737-200 service around the southern part of the continent. Those aircraft will soon be exchanged with new Airbus 320 family types. Owing to the far south location of their homebase, the capital city of Santiago, the requirement for long-haul aircraft has always been a predominant factor. Early models like the B 707 and later DC-10 are no longer in service, and have been replaced by B 767-300s, which in due course will be replaced by A340-300 series aircraft, leaving LanChile as solely an Airbus operator.

The passion for birds and comic legends leads a lot of Japanese aircraft to be painted in very interesting colour schemes. This particular plane belongs to JALways, a subsidiary of Japan Airlines. Photographed in Sendai, Japan, in July 2000, prior to pushback for a domestic flight to Tokyo, is JA8547. Several B 747s and DC-10s operated by Japanese companies are used for domestic services only, to which the very high-density seating is suited. Floor beams and landing gear are strengthened to cope with a higher ratio of landings than their sister ships normally achieve in service. The aircraft here in fact belongs to the international fleet, with a seating allocation of 41 coach and 227 economy class.

Approaching Cancún, Mexico, endless white sandy beaches and crystal-clear water are visible. Located on the eastern side of the Yucatan Peninsula, Cancún has become a major resort, with leading hotel and restaurant chains providing excellent service. During the summer the eastern side of Mexico is often hit by hurricanes, which cause significant damage and delay any flying activity. Winter, as pictured here in January 1996, creates dry air with excellent visibility and flying conditions. Cancún's single runway is 3,500 metres (11,500 feet) long and has instrument approach facilities down to Category 1 minima.

Location: Tenerife-South. Aircraft: MD-11CF. Company: Martinair.

To minimize ground time, this MD-11CF is being refuelled by two trucks at the same time! A wet-lease aircraft flown on behalf of Varig, based in Brazil, this flight runs three times a week between Amsterdam and São Paulo, with a technical stop in Tenerife. Martinair operates two full MD-11 freighter and four convertible freighter versions, allowing it to respond quickly to holiday season demands or ad hoc freight assignments. The MD-11 can carry up to 26 pallets on the upper deck, as well as underfloor cargo. As well as the Douglas aircraft which came as a DC-10 replacement to the Dutch carrier, Martinair flies a single B 757-200, six B 767-300s and three B 747-200 series aircraft, of which one is a full freighter. To boost cargo capacity and services to South America, Martinair signed a strategic alliance with Tampa of Colombia.

Turning off Taxiway A towards the main Terminal Building 1 in Frankfurt, in March 1998, is one of Varig's seven-strong fleet of MD-11s, wearing the old colour scheme. It faces an uncertain future along with its sister ships. The Brazilian aviation industry is facing a difficult time, owing to high inflation and the strength of the US dollar. Varig started jet service 32 years after its launch in 1959, using SE-210 Caravelle aircraft. Boeing 707s, DC-10s and heavy B 747s followed, making Varig the largest carrier in South America. This MD-11 is powered by three GE CF-6-80C2D1F engines, and has a maximum take-off weight of 280–320 kg. The Sel-Cal code is CR-FK.

Malév Hungarian Airlines was founded in 1949 with strong support from the former Soviet Union. Various Russia-built aircraft were subsequently used on routes within the Eastern Bloc, from its home base in Budapest. With the political situation changing in Europe massively over the last two decades, the first Western-built aircraft, a Boeing 737, was bought in 1989. After almost thirty years of service with Malév, the Hungarian carrier phased out its last Tupolev Tu-154 on 29 March 2001. One example is captured here entering the ramp in Rhodes in June 1998. Today the fleet consists of six Fokker 70s, thirteen B 737-300, -400 and -500 series, two B 767-200s and one B 767-300ER which will shortly be returned to the lessor, Pembroke, because of current financial difficulties. This aircraft was used on routes to the Far East.

Singapore Airlines opted for the Airbus 340 to deploy on 'thin' destinations. One example is pictured here, at Athens in July 1998. Seating configuration of the A340 is 10 first, 30 business and 225 economy class, 121 seats fewer than in the company's B 747-400. The maximum take-off weight of Singapore's A340 is currently 275,000 kg. This weight is used not only by the flight crew to determine how much payload and fuel they can carry, but also by airport authorities and air traffic control calculating the landing and overflight fees, respectively! Since the maximum take-off weight can differ for the same aircraft type within the same fleet, air traffic control in certain countries ask the pilots for their aircraft registration. The sole reason is to check the weight they can charge for!

The sky seems to be full of Virgins! But this time it's a Boeing 747-400 bound for Miami. 'Virgin 5' is the callsign and the aircraft is overtaking us 4,000 feet higher, cruising at Mach 0.85. The characteristic sweep of the wing and the bright contrail from the engines makes the Jumbo easy to recognize, even from the ground. Virgin Atlantic currently has 13 B 747-400s in its fleet.

If it comes to striking liveries there is one place on earth you cannot miss, the United States. No matter if it is American Airlines with its metal painted B 737 and B 757 reflecting company history, Continental with its B 777 in the Millennium outfit, Delta with its MD-11 painted in Olympic colours (even UPS did that), or just going back in history with Braniff's 'Big Orange'! Representing the colours of Phoenix and Tuscon is a B 757-257 of America West Airlines. The Arizona Diamondbacks, Phoenix Suns and Cardinals, all sports clubs, are represented on other B 757s as well. Taxiing out at its home base at Phoenix Sky Harbour International Airport in February 1998 is the 76th 757 built by Boeing, N901AW, which left Renton in 1985.

Thundering into the sky out of Zurich and bound for Boston, a few months before the type was disposed in late 1999, is Swissair's B 747-357, HB-IGF. Swissair was the launch customer for the -300 series, the latest 747 development by Boeing at that time. Increased capacity by the stretched upper deck attracted airlines initially, but owing to the increased weight and therefore reduced range – by almost 3,000 km (1,700 miles) – Boeing sold just 80 of the type to various customers, including Saudi, Qantas, KLM and Thai. Seating layouts ranged mostly up to around 500 passengers, with Japan Airlines providing up to 563 seats on their domestic versions! Second-hand demand for the -300 is low, with the first two, an ex-Varig and Sabena type, being converted to freighters and operated by Atlas Air. Singapore Airlines is storing its -300s at Changi Airport and has put them up for sale.

One of the most interesting and beautiful landscapes, untouched nature and clear air can be found in Alaska. Months of complete darkness are followed by continuous sunshine, but temperatures seldom rise above 20°C (71°F), even in the summer of 2000, when we were descending into Anchorage. The strategic location of Alaska, between the Far East and mainland USA, brings many freighter aircraft into Anchorage for refuelling. Cargo volume is so high between the two continents that the heavily laden aircraft, even the B 747-400F, are not able to fly, for example, the Hong Kong–Los Angeles route non-stop, as the passenger version does.

Rotating from Runway 16 at Zurich in July 1999 is Cathay's Airbus 340-313, B-HXD, for another non-stop flight to Hong Kong. Fully laden with fuel, passengers and cargo, almost the full runway length is needed. Terrain and noise prevention require a sharp left turn immediately after departure.

Cathay Pacific's history dates back to 1946, starting with a Douglas DC-3 linking the colony with mainland China and Australia. The Swire Group, which still controls Cathay, took over shortly after the first flights were conducted, leading to more aircraft, such as the Lockheed Electra and Boeing 707. Expansion continued with the arrival of its first wide-body jets, the Lockheed L-1011 TriStar, and later on the Boeing 747-200. Today Cathay operates from the new Chek Lap Kok airport an overwhelming fleet of fifteen A330-300s, fifteen A340-300s, eleven B 777-200 and -300 series, seven B 747-200s and 23 B 747-400 series aircraft. Three classic B 747Fs are operated by Air Hong Kong, and five B 747-300s are leased to Pakistan Airlines. To everyone's surprise, Cathay suddenly stopped all services to Zurich on 30 April 2001.

This B 747-346 belonging to Japan Airlines receives fuel, new catering supplies and maybe a fresh crew, during a hot and humid night in September 1997 in beautiful Bali. Ground times for a wide-body aircraft are around 1½–2 hrs, depending on the amount of fuel it has to carry and the number of passengers. Technical support on outside stations is mostly received from engineering personnel who are employed by the local national carrier, especially if they operate the same aircraft type. In this case it was probably done by Garuda technicians. Bali is located roughly 8 degrees south and 115 degrees east in the Greater Sunda Islands of Indonesia. Flight time from Europe is around sixteen hours, with fuel stops either in the Gulf region or in Colombo. Flights with the national carrier of Indonesia, Garuda, are all routed via the capital, Jakarta.

Founded in July 1980, Aero Lloyd is another privately and bank-owned charter company from Germany. Initial aircraft deployed were three SE-210 Caravelles, serving Turkey, Spain and Greece, mainly from their home base of Frankfurt. Six months later, the first financial difficulties arose, leading to a suspension of activities for two weeks, until many employees offered their own money to continue. In the spring of 1982 three Douglas DC-9-32 series aircraft were bought and the number of destinations increased. More efficient MD-83 and -87 aircraft were acquired for scheduled services, linking four major cities in Germany with London and Paris. Heavy losses quickly accumulated, and Aero Lloyd, with pressure from Lufthansa and British Airways, discontinued those flights. Today the company has settled down to being a well-known operator in the European charter business, and has more or less become an all-Airbus carrier, with seven A320s and twelve A321s, with one more of the latter on order, in its inventory. Seating arrangements are 174, and 210 full coach for the A321. Seen here on the ramp in Corfu in September 1998 is an A320-232 leased from International Finance Corporation.

Wearing only half of the original and colourful Ghana Airways paint scheme is this DC-10-30, OO-PHN (ln84/msn46554), on its final descent into Düsseldorf, Germany. The aircraft has been with several airlines on wet-lease occasions since it was delivered to KLM in 1973. Registered in Belgium, it is currently operated by Skyjet, a company which specializes in ACMI (Aircraft, Crew, Maintenance, Insurance) operations all over the world. Ghana Airways serves Düsseldorf from Accra, via Rome. Further destinations are New York, Amsterdam, London and several major cities in Africa. This shot was taken in January 1998.

High level encounter! This Britannia Boeing 767-304 is overtaking us just 1,000 feet (300 metres) higher above the Atlantic, bound for Orlando on a sunny day in September 1999. You can almost hear the roar of its General Electric engines. Aircraft separation above the North Atlantic has been reduced to 1,000 feet for same-direction flights, so-called RVSM (reduced vertical separation minimum). This reduction will be implemented in early 2002 in certain countries in Europe as well. The pilots of this flight and I exchanged some words on the worldwide air-to-air frequency, and not surprisingly, they took some photos of us as well! Delivered new to the British carrier in May 1996 as G-OBYC, the aircraft was later leased out to Britannia of Germany as D-AGYC.

Starting up engines in the evening sun in May 1999, at its home base of Larnaca, Cyprus, is a Eurocypria A320, registered 5B-DBC. The charter division of Cyprus Airways currently has five models of the type on lease from its mother company, but it is in serious discussions for independence, which would see the Airbuses returned to Cyprus Airways and being replaced by Boeing 737-800 series aircraft. The company's network consists mainly of routes around the eastern Mediterranean and core destinations in Europe. Cyprus Airways itself is currently planning to replace its four Airbus 310s, with the Airbus 330-200 the front-runner to boost capacity on the high-yield route to London.

Lifting off into the sky is an aircraft operated by Virgin Atlantic's sister company Virgin Sun, featuring the appropriate paint scheme. The Airbus 320-214, G-VMED, is one of four A320s that are used on routes from Manchester and Gatwick to Greece, Turkey, Egypt, Italy and the Canary Islands. The location of this shot is Tenerife, the largest of the seven islands. For more than thirty years now these islands, politically belonging to Spain, have been the number one destinations for European holiday-makers, especially from Britain, Scandinavia, Germany and the Netherlands. With their mild climate all year round, it's the perfect spot to go – just four hours away from mainland Europe. Tenerife-South airport is located on the south side of the island, having a single runway 3,200 metres (10,500 feet) long, with instrument approaches installed in each direction. Radar service is excellent, with the majority of approaches flown visually.

Tunisair, the national carrier of Tunisia, brings us back to Africa: this time to Monastir, the third largest city in the country, which has grown to be an attractive tourist destination. With the ground power plugged in, all doors opened and attempting to get some ventilation inside the aircraft – local time is around 19:00 hrs and the temperature still above 40°C (104°F) – this Airbus 319-114 awaits its passengers. Delivered new in August 1998 to the North African carrier, the Airbus 319 is the shortest, so far, aircraft of the 320 family, seating 144 passengers in single-class configuration. Tunisair's fleet is an interesting mix of four B 727-2H3s, four B 737-2H3s, ten Baby Boeing 737-500 and -600 series models, three A319s, twelve A320s and finally three A300B4s, with two of them being 300-600 series, just recently acquired from

Emirates. First flights started in 1948 with help from Air France with a DC-3. The first jet service was operated in 1961, using SE-210 Caravelle aircraft. Today Tunisair's network covers the map substantially in the northern parts of Africa, Morocco, Libya, Algeria, Egypt and into the Middle East. Destinations in Europe are London, Frankfurt, Düsseldorf, Brussels, Geneva, Copenhagen, Amsterdam, Munich, Geneva and Zurich.

Rotating at Faro, Portugal, in July 2000 is TF-ABT, a Lockheed L-1011-100, from the Iceland-based wet-lease specialist, Air Atlanta. Bound for London-Gatwick, the aircraft was operating the summer season for Caledonian. Air Atlanta has become a backbone for many companies whose passenger volume vary considerably with seasonal demands or during the pilgrim season. Comprising a growing number of B 747 classics, Air Atlanta's fleet will exchange its L-1011s for Boeing 767 aircraft, starting in May 2001 with the first set of Boeings, settled under a contract with Excel Airlines. Other customers include Iberia and Saudia. With only 250 TriStar aircraft built between 1970 and 1983, the chance of spotting one in Europe will sadly decrease. The majority are still flying in the United States, but will become increasingly used by Third World countries and also converted for freighter use. Currently some 135 aircraft are in active service.

The flight engineer is counting down the last 50 feet, moments away from touchdown in Las Palmas, Canary Islands. SE-DTC, an L-1011-1 series, is wearing the basic colour scheme of Blue Scandinavia from Sweden. The impressive nose-up attitude, of about 8 degrees, is a characteristic phenomenon of all heavy trijets, including the DC-10 and MD-11. Eastern Airlines and TWA launched the TriStar programme in 1968, with a combined order of almost a hundred aircraft. Delta and Air Canada soon followed. Aircraft orders dropped in the early 1970s following the economic crisis. The -1 series aircraft was followed by a -100 version five years later, having the same dimensions as the original one, but with increased range and maximum take-off weight. This particular aircraft left the plant at Palmdale in November 1973, and was previously operated by Cathay Pacific as VR-HOH.

Shrinking airline bank accounts caused by rising costs of fuel, slumping ticket prices and more competition has led to some airlines using their aircraft as advertising platforms. Ryanair has close tie-ups with a beer company, another carrier with a British car manufacturer, Aero Lloyd is trying to sell sportsgear and even Alitalia was found in the chocolate and watch business, having painted two B 747-200s in a dark blue and the other one in a silver bullet paint scheme. Crossair of Switzerland was the target for the advertising people of a large American fast food chain, resulting in this overall red layout of an MD-83 in July 1999. Rumours that the in-flight catering was changed on this aircraft cannot be confirmed!

The Hawker Siddeley Trident had been flying some twelve months when Boeing launched its rival aircraft in February 1963. Increasing concerns by Boeing that the battle was lost before it even started were quickly dispelled when Eastern, United and Lufthansa ordered substantial numbers right away. The Trident aircraft was basically built for the British market, and did not attract any US airlines, which, at that time anyway, only bought American products. Today the picture is a bit different. Powerplant selection for the B 727-100 was the Pratt & Whitney JT8D, with 14,000 pounds of thrust. A cargo version was quickly developed, enabling carriers to operate the aircraft in a so-called QC (Quick Change) version, where the passenger seats could be taken out in less than 30 minutes, and freight-loaded in, through the forward side-loading door. Seen on finals into Miami in May 1999 is a B 727-281 belonging to Venezuelan carrier Servivensa. This particular aircraft, YV-92C, first flew in 1973.

This view of Greenland on a clear and cold day in March 2000 gives an idea of why airliners used to carry survival equipment. Note the glacier in the lower right corner.

Isolated archipelago in the northern atoll of the Maldive islands. The temperature in the region averages 29 °C (84°F) throughout the year.

One of South America's oldest airlines is Aeropostal from Venezuela, dating back as far as 1930. Receiving service on the ramp in Santo Domingo, the capital of the Dominican Republic, is F-OHPV, an Airbus 310-324, on lease from Airbus Industries Financial Services, hence the French registration. Providing domestic services with nine DC-9-32 and -51 series aircraft, Aeropostal leases several aircraft to cover peak demands during the holiday season. As well as *Papa Victor*, which was photographed in March 1999, the carrier used another A310, an A320 from the defunct Transair and a Boeing 727-200 from Transmeridian on lease. With the high-loading equipment ready at the front cargo door, the aircraft is awaiting its load for the return leg to Caracas.

Having leased out another Airbus 310-222, Airbus Industries is getting heavily involved in remarketing second-hand aircraft to new customers. This time it's line number 334, F-OHPP, built in 1984, and wearing the colours of the national carrier of the Maldives.

With the high-lift devices, or slats, in take-off configuration, the aircraft taxies down the runway at Malé in November 1998, getting ready for a flight to Dubai. Plans were made for other destinations, such as London, Frankfurt, Bangkok and Singapore, but never came to

fruition. The aircraft was subsequently handed back to Airbus. With two Dornier 228s and a single de Havilland Dash 8 left, the airline provides a local service to the neighbouring island of Gan.

Definitely watched by the Atlas Air crew and ourselves, waiting at the holding point of Runway 13 in Abu Dhabi, is this B 707-300C as it smokes in, in November 1997. Belonging to Das Air Cargo of Uganda, the company is managed from its Gatwick base by Cpt. Joe Roy and his wife Daisy. Frequent destinations are Entebbe, Lagos, Accra, Lusaka and Dar es Salaam. Two weekly rotations lead via Bombay to Abu Dhabi or Dubai, and further on to Nairobi. Cargo mainly consists of perishables – fruit and fish – that are flown directly to the large trading malls in Amsterdam. The company's first DC-10-30F, 5X-JOE, was introduced in 1995, an ex-Sabena model, OO-SLA. Two further Douglas freighters were leased in 1995 and 1997.

The stretched B 727, called the -200 series, first flew on 27 July 1967, and could carry a maximum of 189 passengers over a distance of 4,000 km (2,200 miles). Northwest Orient was the launch customer for the latest development, with all the other major carriers in the United States to follow. On the other side of the Atlantic the picture was similar. Air France, Iberia, Lufthansa, Dan Air, TAP, Olympic, Sterling, Hapag-Lloyd, SAT and Turkish Airlines, to name just a few, all operated the aircraft for many years. Today, with strict noise regulations in effect, it has become a rare sight at European airports. The story is different in Latin and South America, where the aircraft is still extremely popular, especially with start-up airlines like Aeromar of the Dominican Republic. Using leased equipment from the American carrier Falcon Air, pictured on page 72, it serves Santo Domingo, Cancún, Puerto Rico and Miami, where this photograph was taken in July 1999.

Dried-out Nile delta in the area of Luxor, Egypt.

Formerly known as Tradewinds Airlines, founded by Singapore Airlines in 1975, this company was renamed Silk Air in 1991. Operating flights throughout South-East Asia brings this A320-232, 9V-SLB, into Phuket, Thailand, on Christmas Eve 1998. Phuket is located one hour south of Bangkok in the Andaman Sea, virtually at the beginning of the famous Strait of Malacca. With its long white sandy beaches, caves and rocks that achieved enormous popularity when they had a starring role in a James Bond film with Roger Moore, and providing excellent Thai cuisine, Phuket has become a very popular hotspot (actually it's my own favourite destination). Flight time from Europe is about twelve hours, with a stop in either Abu Dhabi or Bahrain, depending on the carrier you select, or non-stop service to Bangkok with a connecting flight to Phuket.

Probably one of the most striking liveries is that of Air Jamaica. N630AJ was photographed while on finals into Miami, completing the trip from Montego Bay. Founded in 1968 in connection with Air Canada, Air Jamaica started up with a single DC-9. Services to New York and London were inaugurated with a DC-8, but were discontinued soon afterwards because of low passenger demand. A mixed fleet of Airbus 300/310s, MD-83s and four Boeing 727-200s raised concerns about flexibility and high maintenance costs, so that the management decided to streamline the fleet into an Airbus operation, aquiring the first A320 in 1996, followed by ten more and one A340-300 for long-haul flights to Europe. All aircraft are leased, resulting in numerous US-registered planes being operated, such as N630AJ, named *Ocho Rios*. The company headquarters is located in Kingston.

Another faded glory taxies onto the ramp in Malaga, Spain, on a nice and warm September evening in 1999. No, not Britannia, but the operator that leased the aircraft. Clearly identified by its tail number, EI-TLO belongs to Transair International Airlines from Ireland, which ceased operations in 2000. Specializing in wet-leasing aircraft to a number of operators around the world, its aircraft consisted of eight Airbus 320s and six Airbus 300B4s. Tango Lima Oscar left the Airbus factory as line number 758 in late 1997.

With landing gear retracted and the flaps in take-off configuration, this fully laden B 707-321C, HK-3333X, climbs out of Miami in July 1998 bound for Medellin, Colombia, the home base of TAMPA. Delivered to Pan American as N790PA on 27 February 1964 and converted into freighter configuration in 1977 by the subsequent operator, Avianca, the aircraft saw several other paint schemes, including those of SAM Colombia, TEA of Belgium, Air Atlanta and Florida West, before returning to South America in 1987. TAMPA was founded in 1974, starting operations the same year using a Douglas DC-6, linking Baranquilla with Bogota and Miami. Jet service was introduced in 1980 with two B 707s, of which one was lost while departing Medellin in 1983. Charter flights were briefly conducted to Europe in the 1990s. Today the company basically operates Colombian/US flights, employing this single B 707 and three DC-8-71F aeroplanes. Just recently it unveiled a new, more colourful, paint scheme.

Another colourful British charter carrier's aircraft leaves the main apron at Tenerife in March 2000, heading back to London-Gatwick. Starting out with two Boeing 757-200s in 1987 from its former main base in Manchester, Air 2000 has grown considerably over the last decade. Initial destinations were, as usual, for European holiday-makers, the classics around the Mediterranean. The first long-haul missions went to Kenya and Florida in 1989. The company inaugurated its first A320 in 1992, G-OOAA, coincidentally the aircraft pictured here, powered by two IAE V2500-A1 engines. Later models got the more powerful CFM 56 series engines. Air 2000 currently operates six A320s, six A321s, fourteen B 757-200s and four B 767-300s. Its ICAO callsign is 'Jet Set'.

Operating in its own colours is this B 727-200 of Falcon Air Express, descending into a thundery Miami in August 1999. Founded in 1995, the company flies mainly charter contracts on behalf of tour operators or other smaller airlines around the Caribbean and the southern part of the USA. Since its five B 727s have been sourced from five different airlines, the flight deck and cabin layout may differ slightly from each other. The cockpit of the B 727 features the classic three-man workplace, two pilots and a flight engineer. Because the engines are located at the back, the B 727 cockpit is one of the most quiet ones ever built, with no competition from the B 757 or even the B 747! Since the company I work for has the habit of frequently positioning the crews around Florida and Latin America, the aircraft in question is very often a B 727! On many occasions I was invited to ride on the jump seat in the cockpit, and I definitely enjoyed it.

Framed by Mesopotamia in the west and the mountains in the east is the fascinating area of southern Iran. The two biggest cities in the Zagros mountains are Shiraz and Esfahan, both facing hard climate changes during the year: dry and hot during the summer, with tremendous snowfalls in the winter. Predominating westerly winds have drilled their marks into the mountains over millions of years, resulting in these magnificent structures. Height in this area goes up to 4,500 metres (14,800 feet).

In 1959 three DC-6 aircraft were the first to bear the bright colour scheme of the famous orchid on the tail. Jet service was first introduced with the SE-210 Caravelles and later on DC-9-41s in 1963. Destinations in Asia, into Australia and on trans-Pacific routes were added when the heavy Douglas aircraft, the DC-8 and DC-10, became available. Increasing tourism and cargo business led to the acquisition of the carrier's first B 747-200 in 1979, and although this type is no longer in operation, Thai still has two B 747-3D7s in its fleet. Airbus 300s and 310s are used to cover domestic destinations, as well as connecting Bangkok with nearby major cities like Kuala Lumpur. Thai has become a member of the Star Alliance Group, and operates a fleet of twelve A330-300s, four MD-11s which replaced the DC-10 after almost thirty years of operation, eleven B 737-4D7s, and fourteen B 777s of which eight are -200 series and six are -300s. Fourteen B 747-4D7s are operated mainly on the ultra-

long-haul sector – with one example, HS-TGX, caught on film in Phuket in December 1998 – to cover seasonal demand.

Probably the most striking livery ever painted on a Jumbo is the Tropical Megatop scheme on a Singapore Airlines B 747-412, taxiing to Runway 18 in Frankfurt. Two aircraft got the special markings, 9V-SPL and -SPK, which is photographed here, but tragically it was lost on take-off out of Taipei, bound for Los Angeles on 31 October 2000. Singapore Airlines also received the thousandth B 747 ever built, 9V-SMU, on 13 October 1993. The aerodynamic changes and slight increase of wingspan helped Boeing to reduce fuel burn substantially, and with some extra fuel tanks added, the -400 series range was increased by an incredible 5,000 km (3,000 miles) compared with the -200. Ultra-long-haul sectors crossing the Pacific became possible, eliminating a technical stop in Honolulu. Ironically, just two American companies, Northwest and United, bought the passenger -400 version, with the other big players relying on the Boeing 777 and MD-11 for their long-haul requirements.

While the forward cargo door is being closed and the fuel truck is still connected to Air-India's VT-EJI, an Airbus 310-304, the aircraft is being prepared by the ground staff in Abu Dhabi for its return leg to Mumbai (Bombay) in January 1999. Founded as TATA in 1932, the airline eventually became Air-India in 1946. Starting the jet age very early in the 1960s, and operating the Boeing 747 as one of that company's first customers in 1971, Air-India's network has grown substantially, and now links the two biggest cities in the subcontinent, Delhi and Mumbai, with New York, London, Geneva, Rome, Mauritius, Dubai, Abu Dhabi, Hong Kong, Singapore, Bangkok and Tokyo, to name just a few. The colour scheme sported here is the original one. After a brief change in the early 90s to a more modern look, Air-India changed it back following numerous complaints from its customers.

This photograph was taken some thirty miles from Malé airport during the rainy season in April 1999. The aircraft was just popping out of the first layer of stratus clouds, before a second layer of cumulus clouds was penetrated. Even these smaller formations can cause significant rainfall, to such levels that an approach might have to be abandoned.

The tropical south-west monsoon starts in late April, with the peak activity in August. The dominating factors are the massive high pressure and heat built up over Tibet. It extends westwards into the Arabian Sea and eastwards into the Bay of Bengal. With the Inter-tropical Convergence Zone moving northwards, hot and humid air masses are released, generating heavy rain showers with associated adverse flying conditions. The cloud formation pictured here, just south of Calcutta, seems to have its own tropical depression.

Resting at sunset in Bangkok during the last days of 1997, before we board for a positioning flight to Colombo, is another Cathay Pacific Airbus, this time an A330-300. Cathay used the L-1011 primarily on intra-Asian high-density routes, but when the three-engined workhorse needed replacement, orders were sent to both Toulouse and Seattle. Cathay's network is impressive, basically linking any Asian city with Hong Kong. Fears of Hong Kong losing its identity when China took over in 1997 did not last long, and Cathay's business is better than ever. Local competitor Dragonair, in which Cathay has a stake, also replaced its L-1011s with more economical A330 aircraft in 1995. All Hong Kong-based aircraft were formerly registered VR-xxx, and now have China's ICAO state code B-xxx at the start.

Sobelair was founded in 1946 as a private airline, linking mainly the former Belgian Congo, later Zaire and nowadays called the Democratic Republic of Congo, with Brussels. The initial aircraft used was a DC-4. With national flag carrier Sabena taking control in 1948, all intercontinental flights were suspended, and Sobelair concentrated on flights around Belgium. Travelling by air started to become affordable in the 1960s, and the first jet aircraft, a Caravelle, found its way to Sobelair. With increasing passenger numbers, the need for bigger aircraft resulted in Sabena disposing of some of its B 707s to the charter subsidiary. Recession in the tourist market in Europe forced the company to sell all long-haul aircraft and only operate ex-Sabena B 737-200 series aircraft to destinations around the Mediterranean, before returning to long-haul flights with B 767-300s in 1994. Guided onto the small ramp of Punta Cana, in the Dominican Republic, in February 1998 is OO-STF.

Star Airlines, with its interesting colour scheme, is a French charter operator which was founded in 1995, with operations starting in spring 1997. From its home base at Paris Charles de Gaulle Airport it conducts charter flights throughout Europe, mostly on behalf of tour operator Look Voyages. Pictured here is the first Airbus 320-214, F-GRSD, that was handed over from GATX leasing company to Star Airlines in 1997. Powered by two CFM 56-5B4 engines, it has a maximum take-off weight of 77 tons and seats 180 passengers in full coach configuration. With slats and flaps lowered into take-off position, Sierra Delta leaves the ramp in Malaga, Spain, in September 1999.

With the deregulation of the Turkish charter market, it is almost impossible to catch up with all the new airlines. Sitting idle on the tarmac in Antalya, Southern Turkey, in April 1999 is TC-ALN, an A300B4-103 which left the French manufacturer in 1978 (msn065). The high-density seating of the Airbus 300 models has proved the right choice for many other Turkish companies, whose airliners can be spotted daily at any major airport in Germany. Powered by two General Electric CF6-50 engines, the aircraft has a maximum take-off weight of 157,500 kg, and so belongs to the wake turbulence category 'Heavy'!

Head on! Undoubtedly a Virgin Airbus 340-300, over the North Atlantic heading eastwards in April 1999. With the launch of the first 'Big European' by Lufthansa in January 1993, Airbus entered an era so far reserved for Boeing: ultra-long-haul capability, combining the very latest technology with a high standard of efficiency, safety and comfort, enabling carriers to cover routes which were economically nonsense to operate with a Boeing 747, because of low passenger demands on the one hand and not being in the non-stop range of a twin-engined aircraft on the other. The B 777 was not on the market at that time, and the MD-11 did not meet performance criteria promised by Douglas. A big blow to the American manufacturer came when Singapore Airlines, for exactly that reason, cancelled its MD-11 orders and switched to the Airbus 340 to allow it to fly a non-stop service from Singapore to Paris, a route which is critical during the northern winter, owing to the predominating strong westerly headwinds. The A340-200 broke the world record on 16 June 1993 when it departed Paris and flew around the world in 48 hrs 22 minutes with just one fuel stop in Auckland, New Zealand.

The first variant of the B 747, the -100 series, took to the air on 9 February 1969, entering, along with four sister ships, a tremendous testing programme for certification. The launch customer was Pan American, followed by TWA and Lufthansa. Boeing quickly realized the need for improvement, in terms of range and subsequently take-off weight, and the more powerful -200 series left the plant in Everett in November 1970.

The easiest way to distinguish the -100 series from the -200 is the number of windows in the upper deck, with the older version having three and the -200 having ten. Parked on the ramp in Athens in June 1998 is one of the oldest B 747-146s still flying: N703CK (ln54/msn19727), delivered new to Japan Airlines in 1970, but now wearing the bright colour scheme of American International Airways, formerly known as Kalitta Flying Service, and today already absorbed into Kitty Hawk. The main operating field is the cargo sector, with numerous DC-8, L-1011 and Boeing 747 aircraft used. Two B 747s are in passenger configuration, mainly flying full charter contracts on behalf of the US government, like this 476-seater variant.

Founded in 1993, Polar Air Cargo started flying, from its home base in Los Angeles, with two leased B 747-100 freighters on behalf of UPS and FedEx. The number of aircraft has risen sharply within the last nine years. Today Polar Air Cargo has a fleet of thirteen B 747-100 series, five B 747-200s, the brand-new -400 F, with four examples in operation and one more on order. The company's network covers Miami, Chicago, Atlanta, New York, Honolulu, Taipei, Manila, Tokyo, Hong Kong, Melbourne, Auckland, Sydney, Prestwick, Helsinki, Amsterdam, Rio de Janeiro, Manaus, Santiago de Chile and São Paulo.

Starting with some borrowed money in 1971, the idea of overnight express delivery was born, but the result was almost a disaster. Frederick W. Smith and a handful of employees even spent their own money to buy fuel for the trucks and planes, just to keep going. Today FedEx employs more than 150,000 people worldwide and uses some 650 aircraft. Lining up on Runway 9R in Miami is a FedEx DC-10-30 series aircraft in the company's new livery, which was introduced in l994. FedEx operates 92 DC-10 aircraft, both -10 and -30 series, along with its strong and still growing fleet of MD-11 aircraft, on a worldwide cargo network from its main base in Memphis, Tennessee. A massive fleet of small turboprops, Boeing 727Fs as well as Airbus 300-600s and 310s, act as feeder aircraft throughout the USA, Europe and the Far East. Boeing currently offers a conversion kit to DC-10 operators, with FedEx leading the programme, which covers a major flight deck upgrade. LCD displays and enhanced navigation equipment eliminate the flight engineer's position. The aircraft is called the Boeing MD-10.

Clear arctic cold air generated a
magnificent view over the French Alps
in February 1999.

El Al's operations were started in 1949 with a Curtiss C-46 and a DC-4 aircraft out of Tel Aviv, the airline's home base. The first jet was bought in 1960, a B 707, and since that time the carrier has never had anything but Boeing equipment in its hangars. The first B 747 joined in 1971, replacing the B 707 on the Tel Aviv–London–New York route, which is the most lucrative destination for El Al. Pure cargo services were launched in 1975 with the company's first receipt of a B 747-258C. Three more of the type, including a full freighter, were added in the following years. In 1983 the ageing

B 707s were replaced by more economical B 767-258s. In 1999 El Al ordered three Airbus 330-200s to replace the classic B 747s, which had already been supported by four new B 747-458s, but a massive protest from the US government forced El Al to cancel the order and instead opt for three B 777-200s.

About to depart Runway 33R in Athens in June 1998 is one of El Al's first B 757-258s, 4X-EBM, delivered in 1987. Wearing the old colour scheme, the B 757 will be replaced by the new-generation B 737, of which four have already been delivered.

Eyed by three single-engined aircraft, the shadow sinks into the runway on a beautiful day in October 2000 at Paderborn airfield, located more or less in the middle of Germany. Waiting at the holding point of Runway 06, they have to wait a bit longer to get their take-off clearance, since our aircraft, a Boeing 757 (I am sure you have guessed it already from the shadow), belongs to the 'Heavy' wake turbulence category . The Boeing 757 is the only aircraft in the world where the maximum take-off weight, which is normally used to determine the aircraft's category, was slashed in response to the numerous accidents that happened to aircraft departing or landing too close behind it. Landing separation behind a B 757 is five nautical miles. Paderborn airfield has an elevation of 213 metres (699 feet) and a runway length of 2,180 metres (7,152 feet).

Compania Mexicana de Aviaçon has now been in business for 77 years, with Pan American having the major share up to 1968. DC-3 and DC-6 aircraft were used to connect Mexico City with Acapulco, Havana, Kingston, Managua, Houston, Los Angeles and the capitals in South America. In 1966 the Boeing 727 was introduced, after some initial jet trials with the de Havilland Comet did not work out. A special DC-10-15 version was launched by the Douglas company, especially designed for Aeromexico and Mexicana to operate from hot and high airports, such as their home base Mexico City, beginning in 1981. Restructuring plans came up in the early 1990s with the disposal of the wide-bodies and some loss-making destinations. Today Mexicana is in the process of changing its whole fleet, adding the A320 series and some Fokker 100 aircraft. The future of its seven Boeing 757s, which replaced the DC-10, remains unclear. Lining up on Runway 9R at Miami in July 1998, bound for Cancún, Mexico, is XA-MEH, Nuevo Laredo, a B 727-264 bought new in 1980.

More than 1,800 Boeing 727s were built until 1984, when production ended, and the vast majority are still flying! Delta and American operate high numbers of the passenger version, and a rising number are being operated in Latin and South America. South-East Asia is more or less a B 727 no-fly zone, with the Middle East having, not counting the VIP aircraft, just three operators left – Yemenia, Ariana Afghan and Air Gulf Falcon. On the African continent, countries like Angola, the Democratic Republic of Congo and South Africa use the most B 727s, interestingly with a lot of -100 series versions. Express giants UPS and DHL have many of their

classic workhorses based in Europe, hush-kitted to cope with Stage 3 noise regulations. Flying on behalf of the major parcel carriers is Amerijet International of Ft Lauderdale in Florida, connecting the tiny islands of Antigua, Saint Maarten, St Lucia, Curaçao, Tobago and Barbados with the major hubs. Caught on film in June 1999 is N395AJ, a B 727-233F, approaching Miami International Airport.

In the mid-1970s Boeing started to look for a B 727 replacement, with several options made public during the Paris Air Show in 1975, starting with a stretched version called B 727-300, to a twin-engine with T-tail configuration, up to a three-engined T-tail version, already called B 777. Owing to lack of interest from the airlines, all plans were shelved in favour of a completely new design. In 1978 the B 757 finally emerged from the drawing board, with British Airways and Eastern Airlines placing the initial orders while still four years ahead of the maiden flight. A new advanced cockpit technology was used for the first time, the flight engineer was dumped and bigger, more efficient and less noisy engines were fitted. Fuel consumption is 16 per cent better than the classic B 727, and take-off and landing performance significantly

improved. Iberia is a long-time B 727 operator, in fact the only flag carrier in Europe that still flies the B 727. So it was more than obvious that the Spanish company would opt for the B 757 as

well, despite also having A320s in its fleet. Pushing back from the gate in Malaga, during a cold January morning in 1999, is one of its B 757-256s for the early run back to Madrid.

A Boeing 757 sales tour to South America, Africa, Europe and South-East Asia was launched in late 1982, covering 46,000 miles, with no aircraft defects at all. Some winter and high-wind operations could be tested during the visit to Scandinavia. Sales in Asia were very low, with only Singapore Airlines placing an order, but it does not operate the type any longer. Typical Asian wide-body demand was the reason for Airbus winning the race with its A300 series, which dominates the region in the short and medium sector. A few B 757s found their way there later, with Royal Nepal, Royal Brunei and airlines in mainland China operating the type. With the former Soviet Union becoming more

'westernized', some Boeing aircraft were leased by several Russian operators. One of them is Moscow-based Transaero. Next to some B 737s and a DC-10 that was leased from American Airlines

recently, Transaero operated five Boeing 757-200s leased from GE Capital and ILFC. Getting ready to depart Frankfurt in February 1998 is N701LF, a B 757-28A powered by Rolls-Royce powerplants.

In 1984 the first B 737-300 made its maiden flight from Boeing Field in Seattle. With newly developed CFM 56 engines providing more power, and a massive noise reduction and advanced new glass cockpit elements, the -300 version became an absolute best seller. The fuselage was increased by 3 metres (10 feet), and can accommodate up to 148 passengers in a single-class layout. Photographed here, in a striking blue livery, is B 737-33A, OK-FUN, from the Czech charter operator Fischer Air, just moments before pushback at Antalya, Turkey, in October 1999.

A 'build-up' over Turkey in the late evening in September 1997. Even isolated thunderclouds must be avoided at all times, since massive turbulence and hail inside can cause structural overload to the aircraft. These clouds develop, mostly in the afternoon, when enough heat is generated and unstable moist air is present. In the early days of aviation, when airborne weather radar was not available, such thunderclouds were hard to avoid.

The requirement for Boeing to develop a shortened version of the B 747-200, capable of flying ultra-long-haul flights, came up when several airlines switched to Douglas and Lockheed to buy DC-10s and TriStars for medium-density work, where the B 707 was too small and the B 747 too big. The official go-ahead was given in August 1973 to proceed with the development of the B 747SP, Special Performance. Lacking any orders, Boeing was taking a big financial risk, but the gamble paid off when Pan American ordered ten B 747SPs in September 1973. With Boeing Chief Test pilot Jack Waddell at the controls, the maiden flight was made on 4 July 1975 – Independence Day. Success never came, and Boeing sold only 45 aircraft of this type. Barely seen in airline service any more, one third are stored in the desert and another third are being converted into VIP aircraft. Corsair of France in fact has still got its single B 747SP, F-GTOM (ln293/msn21253) on active duty. It is pictured in March 1999 on the ramp in Santo Domingo, Dominican Republic, arriving from Paris Charles de Gaulle. The aircraft was originally delivered to South African Airlines as ZS-SPD before being sold to Royal Air Maroc as CN-RMS and finally to Corsair. An interim registration in Luxembourg, LX-ACO, was used until the B 747SP was certified in France.

A European flag carrier with a long history is Madrid-based Iberia. Illustrated here is the company's B 747-256, EC-DNP, named *Juan Ramon Jimenez*, leaving the runway in Miami after completion of another long run from the Spanish capital. Iberia uses Miami as a major hub for its destinations in Latin America and the Caribbean. Traditionally linked with South America, Iberia has based a couple of its own DC-9 aircraft in Miami, acting as feeder aircraft between San Salvador, Guatemala City, Cancún, Mérida, Barranquilla and Managua to get maximum seating on the B 747 out of Miami. The major cities in the area, such as Havana, Bogota, Caraccas, Buenos Aires and Mexico City, have direct connections to Madrid. The B 747 is supported by fifteen Airbus 340-300 series aeroplanes.

No, it's not a Boeing 757 with winglets caught somewhere in the desert on test flights! It's a Tupolev Tu-204-120, SU-EAF, wearing Air Cairo titles and landing at Luxor in December 1999. The maiden flight for one of the latest developments of Russian-built technology was on 2 January 1989. Its external dimensions are very close to the B 757-200, but with Russian Solowjew PS-90A engines mounted under the wing, performance was anything but impressive. The same number of passengers could be carried as in the B 757, but the range was not even half the distance the American model could do. In 1991 Tupolev decided to mount the more powerful Rolls-Royce RB-211-535E4, the model that powers most of the B 757s worldwide, onto the aircraft to boost sales. Air Cairo currently operates six of the type, including one freighter version. All aircraft are powered by Rolls-Royce powerplants.

Since the vast majority of airline liveries have white as the basic colour, this unique paint scheme is a real eye-catcher. Painted onto a Blue Scandinavia B 757-236, SE-DUP, it reflects the national colours of Sweden, blue and yellow. From its home base at Stockholm-Arlanda Airport, the company used to fly charter work on behalf of the Transwede Group, before it was merged into Britannia Airways in 1998. Known as Britannia Sweden now, the carrier retained its ICAO callsign, 'Blue Scan'. The fleet consists of three Boeing 737-800s, four B 757-200s and a single B 767-300ER at present, all painted in Britannia livery, but with their former Swedish registration still recognizable. Leaving the ramp in Las Palmas in January 1998 is former Air 2000 G-OOOT, powered by two Rolls-Royce RB-211 engines and manufactured in 1990.

Deployed reversers decelerate this B 757-28A during its landing roll on Runway 24L in Palma de Mallorca in August 1998, arriving from Manchester. The black, red and yellow markings remind me of a German outfit, but represent the scheme of the British charter company Flying Colours. Start-up was in February 1997 with its first B 757, G-FCLA, the one captured here! A further five were added from the leasing companies ILFC and GATX, in a typical British seating configuration of 235 single-class, the maximum possible in a B 757-200. Destinations have been the sunshine countries around the Mediterranean. In 1999 Flying Colours and British Caledonian merged into JMC. Now wearing the green and blue cheatline of the new company, all ex-Flying Colour aircraft have retained their old registrations. JMC recently took delivery of its first B 757-300.

Main gear touchdown and reverser deployed brings N306GB *Sir George* back to its home base of Miami, on a bright morning in May 1999, returning from Latin America. This L-1011-200 was converted by Marshall Aerospace into a full freighter. The L-1011 is becoming extremely popular for conversion, which extends the life of this great aircraft for at least another twenty years. Starting out with a bunch of Boeing 707s, which were later all exchanged for DC-8, -50 and -60 series, Arrow Air has become a major player in the freight sector, especially the time-related perishable market between the USA and South America. In 2000, the carrier merged with Fine Air, another Miami-based cargo carrier, also featured in this volume (see page 102), making it the largest cargo mover at the gateway to South America. The example photographed here was previously operated by Gulf Air as A40-TY.

Two isolated thunderclouds over Wyoming in July 1996 which are already beyond their mature stage and will disappear soon. Large cold fronts in the central part of the United States very often create hazardous weather, resulting in the largest number of tornado strikes in the world. Since there is no natural obstacle, such as mountains, to prevent cold air masses flowing from Canada southwards and meeting hot and humid air generated in the Gulf of Mexico, this area is also called Tornado Alley.

The largest B 747 cargo operator is Atlas Air, based in New York. Founded in 1992 by the late Michael Chowdry, who tragically died in 2000 in an aeroplane accident, the company has specialized in long-term wet-lease arrangements with major flag carriers, like British Airways, China Airlines, Emirates and Lufthansa. Roll-out of the first -400 freighter was in May 1993, and it was handed over to Europe's number one all-cargo operator, Cargolux. A maximum of 113,000 kg can be carried over a distance of 8,000 km (4,300 miles). Externally the -400 freighter can be distinguished by its short upper deck also found on the -200 series, and by the fuel-saving winglets. The upper deck has only three windows and is used as a crew rest facility. Pictured here, on the Boeing ramp in Everett in September 1998, is N493MC, as it is getting prepared for delivery. Atlas Air currently operates 24 classic Jumbos and twelve new B 747-47UF aircraft.

This aircraft is being guided by the marshaller into the tiny ramp at Punta Cana, Dominican Republic, in November 1997. Air Transat's TriStar C-FTNB, a converted -150 series, was originally delivered to Eastern Airlines as N309EA in 1972. Viewed from our cockpit, the parking situation on this airfield gets difficult if two wide-body aircraft are already sitting on the ground. The second marshaller is not visible in this shot, but is absolutely necessary to provide wing-tip clearance on the inbound turn. Founded in 1987, Air Transat quickly became the largest charter operator in Canada. Operating five B 757-200s, three Airbus 330s and up to fifteen L-1011s of any series from its home base in Montreal, the company is not anxious to continue to fly the L-1011 for another couple of years. It has recently bought two -500s from AirLanka, ex-4R-ULA and -ULB. Other derivatives have come from Cathay, Eastern and TAP.

In the 1950s Boeing was approached by the US military for a replacement aircraft for its ageing KC-97 Stratotanker. Various proposals had been made, but still did not satisfy either the military or the airlines, when finally a new design emerged from the drawing board. The prototype, N70700, first flew on 15 May 1954 with 'Tex' Johnston at the controls. Travel time between New York and Los Angeles was almost cut in half, which so impressed airline managers that Pan

American ordered a massive number of Boeing 707s, later totalling 124 aircraft in their fleet. To convince European airlines of the new jet age, Boeing demonstrated the first non-stop over-the-Pole flight in a B 707 on 2 May 1959 from Seattle to Rome. With more records broken later on, not surprisingly many governments opted for the Boeing 707 as head-of-state aircraft and in the tanker/cargo role, including Germany, which bought four -320 series aircraft. Idle on the ground in Mombasa

in September 1994, during the Somali crisis, is msn19999, registered 10+03 from the German Air Force. The aircraft was delivered on 31 October 1968 and flew for more than thirty years on behalf of the Air Force, before it was sold in 1999 to Air Gulf Falcon of Sharjah, UAE, registered 5Y-GFF. Recently it was sold on to a new Sudanese company called Spirit of Africa, and now wears ST-AQI on its fuselage.

The German charter carrier Air-Berlin links smaller airports in Germany, like Münster-Osnabrück, Paderborn and Dortmund, with the main holiday destinations around the Mediterranean Sea, and has been aggressively expanding over recent years. Controlled from its main base in Berlin, the carrier's current fleet of six B 737-400 series and, twenty -800 series, with another six on order, are heavily utilized in airports in the former Eastern Germany as well, as these airports do not have any night-time restrictions on operations. Leaving the ramp in Fuerteventura, Canary Islands, is D-ABAL, built in 1996, with a seating configuration of 167 straight economy.

Another newcomer in the heavily competitive German charter market is Hamburg International. Founded in 1998 by German and Chilean businessmen, it leased two Boeing 737-700s from Pembroke Capital. To cope with the low winter season in Europe, one aircraft was ferried to Chile in winter 2000/01 to fly throughout the Caribbean, with Hamburg/Chile stickers painted on the fuselage. Although the basic paint scheme reminds me somewhat of Lufthansa, I am not aware of any connection with that company. Photographed here is D-ASKH in April 1999, at the Germans' number one holiday destination, Mallorca.

A cumulo-nimbus over southern Germany in the summer of 1995 on descent into Frankfurt. Note the spread-out at the top of the cloud, clearly indicating the boundary layer between the air mass and the tropopause, where a temperature conversion takes place.

Who bites whom in this dramatic head-on shot of a Malaysian Boeing 777-2H6 leaving the main apron in Munich in June 1998! The massive Rolls-Royce Trent engines on the B 777 almost seem to devour the small Canadair jet ahead of us. Providing daily flights from Kuala Lumpur to Munich, Malaysian Air Systems is another carrier from South-East Asia that opted early for the new 777, despite having ten A330-300 aircraft in its inventory, which are mainly used on inter-Asian trunk routes, such as Kuala Lumpur to Hong Kong and Bangkok. Neighbouring rivals Thai, Cathay and Singapore Airlines also fly a mixed fleet of Airbus and Boeing products.

Founded in 1992, Fine Air operates a scheduled cargo network linking Miami with numerous points within the Caribbean and South America. Frequent destinations cover Providenciales, Grand Turk, San Juan, Managua, San José, Panama, Quito, Tegucigalpa and Guayaquil, as well as strategic points in mainland USA – Los Angeles and Houston for example. The cargo mainly consists of consumer goods on the southbound sector and of flowers and vegetables on the return trip. On short final into Santo Domingo, in the Dominican Republic, in March 1999 is N30UA, a DC-8-61F powered by four Pratt & Whitney JT3-3B engines, which have been hush-kitted to meet ICAO Stage 3 noise regulations, enabling the carrier to conduct charter assignments to very noise-sensitive destinations anywhere in the world. This particular aircraft was delivered new to United Airlines in 1967, and had seen many operators before finally joining Fine Air. The two -61 series planes were joined by seven -54 series, one -55 series and three -51 converted aircraft. A single L-1011-200F was bought from the defunct Millon Air in 1997, N851MA, which was operated by LTU. Fine Air merged, as previously stated, with Arrow Air, bringing together an impressive fleet of Douglas and Lockheed aircraft.

Angel Air's B 737-5H6, 9M-MFE, was photographed with the gear down and the flaps in landing configuration, moments from touchdown in Phuket, Thailand. This Bangkok-based airline used a single -500 series on a brief lease from Malaysian Airlines in late 1998. The shortest version of Boeing's first new-generation 737 is just 0.3 metre (1 foot) longer than the original -200 series. The 2,000th-built B 737 in fact was a -500 version and was delivered to Lufthansa in 1991.

Welcome to the jungle! This photograph was taken during the descent into Colombo International Airport after a huge thunderstorm had passed through. Note the river that has turned from the normal green and blue into brown, while the mud around has liquefied owing to the associated heavy rain. The intensity of rainfall in the tropics differs considerably from what we are used to in Europe.

'Lufthansa 462 cleared to land.' Moments from touchdown at Miami's International Airport is a Lufthansa B 747-230 linking Frankfurt daily with the Sunshine State. The German flag carrier has now retired all its classic B 747 passenger-versions and keeps ten pure freighter Jumbos flying.

Reorganized after the Second World War, Lufthansa started flying again in 1954, using a Convair 340. The jet age was introduced in 1960 with the Boeing 707 on services to the Middle East, Africa and the United States. The Boeing 727 and 737 followed, building up a comprehensive route structure across

Europe. DC-10s and Airbus 300 series were added later to cover the increasing demand on medium-density, long-haul sectors, as well as intra-German services, linking Frankfurt with Hamburg and Munich. Featured here is ln665/msn23622, D-ABZH, delivered in February 1987.

Originally planning a stretched version of the B 767, the Seattle-based aircraft manufacturer opted for a completely new design, the Boeing 777. Working closely with a group representing major prospective customer airlines, Boeing officially launched the B 777 programme in 1989. A new wing was designed round a nine-abreast fuselage, giving it a seating capacity of around 400 passengers and an initial range up to 4,500 nm. The flight deck features the latest technology, including collision avoidance and GPS. United Airlines became the launch customer for the Boeing 777-200 in 1995. Photographed here is the first stretch version, the -300. Slightly longer than the old giant, the B 747-400, it is currently the longest twin-engined aircraft in the world. The aircraft is wearing the company colours of Boeing. It was used as a test bed in September 1998 from the company's plant at Paine Field, Everett, where the B 747, 767 and 777 are built.

Commencing pushback prior to an acceptance flight from the Boeing company is Lauda Air's OE-LPB, B 777-2Z9, named after the famous author Ernest Hemingway. Former Formula One ace Niki Lauda ordered four Boeing 777s powered by General Electric powerplants in 1991, which are currently deployed on routes to Kuala Lumpur, Hong Kong, Sydney, Miami and Los Angeles. During high-season demands in summer the aircraft are also seen at destinations around Spain and Greece. Employing its own chief cooks on certain routes, exclusively for the first-class passengers, Lauda Air has won several prizes for best catering and in-flight entertainment in its category. Austrian Airlines and Lufthansa recently took control of the airline.

One of the first Boeing 777 customers was Dubai-based Emirates. Founded in 1985 and headed by HH Sheikh Ahmed bin Saeed Al Maktoum, Emirates has seen a tremendous growth in the last few years. Originally it started with a couple of used B 727-200s, and now has one of the youngest fleets on earth. The thirteen-strong fleet of B 777 aircraft, both -200 and -300 series, is currently supplemented by ten Airbus 330-243s, with another eight on order, and five Airbus 340-541s also ordered. Thirteen elderly A300 and 310 series are being phased out as the new aircraft arrive. Emirates placed an order for the new A380 as well, this time in full freighter configuration. The only full freighter aircraft currently employed is a single B 747-400F, leased from wet-lease specialist Atlas Air. The aircraft is painted in full Emirates livery and flies regular services between Amsterdam, Dubai and Hong Kong. Seen here getting ready for another sortie is a B 777-21H, leaving the gate in Colombo for connecting services to Singapore.

To cover low utilization of short- and medium-range aircraft during the European winter, many British companies lease out their aircraft, including crews, to tour operators. This results in interesting paint schemes.

This example, G-BXKA, an Airbus 320-214, is flying on behalf of American operator Apple Vacations, with the aircraft handled by British charter carrier JMC, hence the basic colour scheme. Resting at the gate in beautiful

and sunny Cancún, Mexico, prior to departure to New York during March 2000 is line number 714, an example previously flown by America West as N714AW.

Leaving Runway 18 at Malé in November 1998, after a straight-in approach from Bangalore, is an Airbus 320-231 from India's national carrier, Indian Airlines. Its history goes back to 1953, with the Indian government taking control of the airline business, forcing all

privately owned companies to accept state control and combining them into just two airlines, Air-India and Indian Airlines. With Air-India doing all the long-haul operations, Indian Airlines offers domestic services around the subcontinent. Destinations outside India

include Karachi, Lahore, Kathmandu, Colombo, Chittagong, Dhaka, Malé and Kabul. Indian Airlines hit the headlines in 1998 when one of its eleven-strong fleet of A300B2 and B4 aircraft was hijacked and finally stormed in Dubai, after a three-day ordeal around the Gulf.

Stormy approach into Denpasar-Bali, Indonesia, during the high season of the monsoon in 1996. Flying in South-East Asia requires a thorough knowledge of weather in terms of fuel planning and alternative airports available. Clouds can go up to 57,000 feet in this part of the world.

Formerly known as TEA Basel, the Swiss charter company changed its name to TEA Switzerland before later being controlled by easyJet. Leaving the ramp in Palma de Mallorca in April 1998 is HB-IIH, a B 737-7Q8. The second set of 'new-generation' 737s are dubbed 600/700/800 series. With another upgrade on avionics, an engine with better fuel economy and therefore a further reduction in direct operating costs, airlines placed massive orders even before it was officially launched. The aircraft can accommodate 144 passengers in single-class configuration, with its bigger sister ship, the -800, having up to 189 seats.

MD-11 operator, LTU International Airways, was founded in 1955. Four MD-11s were ordered in the 1980s as replacements for the L-1011 TriStar. From its home base in Düsseldorf, Germany, the company flies regular services to the Mediterranean; Africa; North, Central and South America; the Caribbean; the Middle and Far East; besides Sri Lanka and the Maldives. Worldwide charter assignments are on the agenda as well. LTU will replace its present fleet of twelve Boeing 757 and six Boeing 767 aircraft with an all-Airbus fleet, comprising the A320/321 and A330-200/300 versions. The location of this shot is Agadir, Morocco, in May 1998. D-AERZ, line number 533, was the last MD-11 that was delivered to LTU. It now flies with Swissair as HB-IWU and is earmarked for FedEx freighter conversion in May 2003.

Flights commencing in 1983, America West has seen tremendous growth. Soon leaving the Arizona–Nevada–New Mexico triangle with the introduction of the Boeing 747-200, it conducted high-load flights from Canada into newly booming Las Vegas, which was developing new theme hotels like the Luxor and MGM Grand, and attractions such as little Paris and Venice. Increasing competition threatened

Jumbo operations and they were finally cancelled when America West had to apply for Chapter 11 protection in 1991. Smaller aircraft joined the fleet, and destinations again concentrated around the sunny states in the south-west. Financial recovery was achieved in 1996 when Mesa Airlines bought a stake in the carrier, which led to the introduction of the Canadair Regionaljet. America West's fleet today

comprises fourteen B 737-200s, 50 B 737-300s and thirteen B 757-200s. The B 737s are progressively being exchanged for the Airbus 320-family series, with 68 delivered and another 26 on order. Wearing the company's new livery are a B 737-300 and an America West Express Canadair jet at Sky Harbour International Airport in February 1998.

INDEX